WAITER, THERE'S A TIE IN MY SOUP

Also by Gary Wise and Lance Aldrich

It's a Dog-Eat-Garbage World

Andrews and McMeel
A Universal Press Syndicate Company
Kansas City

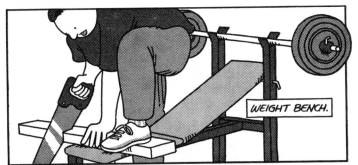

WEIGHT BENCH.

ROWING MACHINE.

EXERCISE BIKE.

TREADMILL.

WISE/ALDRICH

WHO SAYS EXERCISE EQUIPMENT NEVER GETS USED?

How high does that roofing estimate seem now?

The business presentation: unintentional stand-up comedy.

Big Beefy Boy and Heap-O-Fries: If your IQ were as high as your cholesterol, you'd know better.

Why jog out in the fresh air when you can spend $3,000 and do it in the basement?

How to remove that unsightly lump from your couch.

Among the real joys of parenthood are those little walks with the children.

8

**600,000 movies nobody ever rents.
Six movies that are always out.**

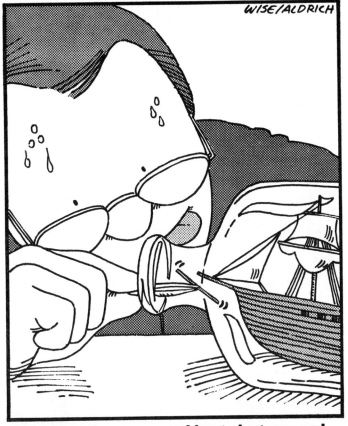

**Hobbies give you something to be tense and
irritable about when you're away from work.**

9

**The first time you're offered a
senior citizen discount.**

**In the event of a bank robbery,
at least the pens will be safe.**

10

DON'T CROSS
YOUR MOTHER.
SHE HAS YOUR
BABY PICTURES
AND SHE'S NOT
AFRAID TO
USE THEM.

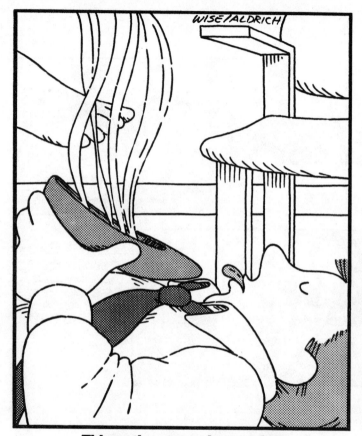

Things they try to keep quiet
in shoe salesman school.

Chances are, your life is not going to be
the subject of intense interest to the
supermarket tabloids.

General Rule No. 1: If you do not have cows, you should not have a cowboy hat.

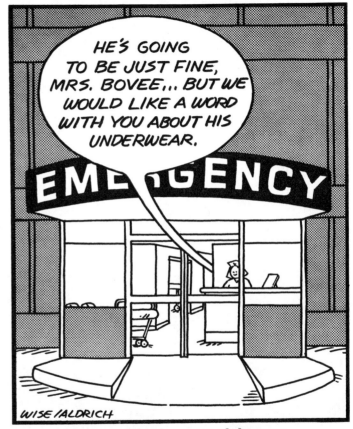

Your mother's worst nightmare.

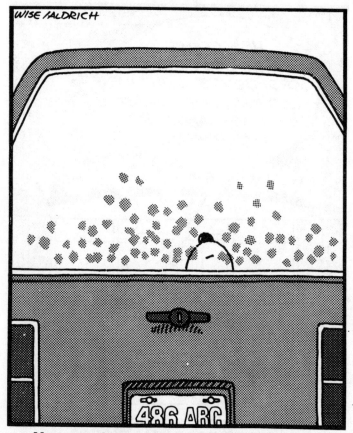

You can always tell a dog owner's vehicle by the nose prints on the windows.

A tool that tells you exactly how far off you were when you cut whatever it was you just cut.

Your favorite sports team probably doesn't mope around when you have a bad day the way you do when they have one.

16

Okra isn't the only thing that looks unappetizing on a plate.

Technically, it's body building. It's just a different kind of body being built.

Intelligent as cats are, there are still some concepts they fail to grasp.

Dilemma.

Lifestyles of the not rich and not famous.

**Things you know exist but can't prove:
the Door Ding Fairy.**

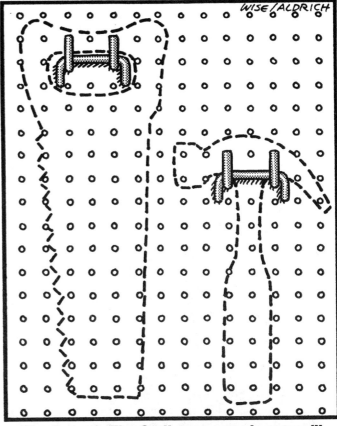

**Handyman's Tip: Outline your tools so you'll
know what you can't find and where the new
one goes until you lose that one, too.**

19

The only trouble with last year's pants is that they have to fit this year's butt.

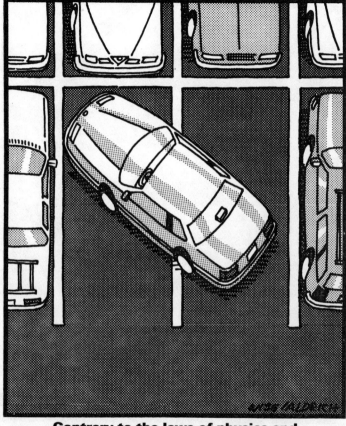

Contrary to the laws of physics and common courtesy, it is possible to be in two places at once.

SOFT MUSIC.

CANDLELIGHT.

A VINTAGE WINE.

A SWELL DINNER.

A COZY FIRE IN THE FIREPLACE WITH THE FLUE STUCK CLOSED.

SOME ENCHANTED EVENING, YOU MAY MEET A FIREMAN.

Static cling: the ignominy of being attacked by your own pants.

Unfortunately, the best cure for cold feet is a warm leg.

22

Home handyman tip: Left uncleaned, that $19 professional-quality natural-bristle brush makes a dandy hammer.

WISE/ALDRICH

$$\sqrt{v^2 \pm a^2}\, dv = \frac{v}{2}\sqrt{v^2 \pm a^2} \pm \frac{a^2}{2} + C$$

$$\ln|v + \sqrt{v^2 \pm a^2}| + C \quad \frac{\sqrt{v^2 + a^2}}{v}$$

$$dv = \sqrt{v^2 + a^2} - a\,\ln\left(\frac{a + \sqrt{v^2 + a^2}}{v}\right)$$

$$v^2\sqrt{v^2 \pm a^2}\, dv = \frac{v}{8}(2v^2 \pm a^2)$$

$$\sqrt{v^2 \pm a^2} - \frac{a^4}{8}\ln|v + \sqrt{v^2 \pm a^2}| + C$$

$$\frac{v^2\, dv}{\sqrt{v^2 \pm a^2}} = \frac{v}{2}\sqrt{v^2 \pm a^2} \pm \frac{a^2}{2}\ln|v$$

$$\frac{dv}{v^2\sqrt{v^2 \pm a^2}} = \pm\frac{\sqrt{v^2 \pm a^2}}{a^2 v} + C\,(v^2 \pm a^2)$$

$$(v^2 \pm a^2)^{3/2}\, dv = \frac{v}{8}(2v^2 \pm 5a^2) = \rbrack\lbrack$$

WISE/ALDRICH

The formula for finding where to put the nail to hang the picture.

23

Your contractor as a child.

A question best left unanswered until you get
a good look at the guy driving the truck.

24

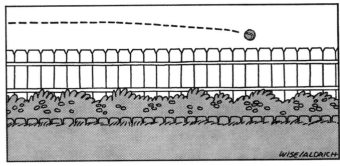

WISE/ALDRICH

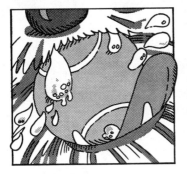

IT'S NOT
SO MUCH THAT
THEY ENJOY
FETCHING IT.
WHAT THEY
ENJOY IS
WATCHING YOU
TOUCH IT WHEN
THEY BRING
IT BACK.

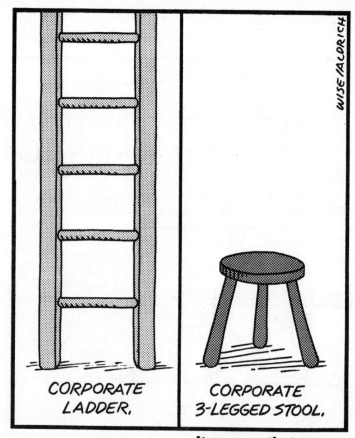

CORPORATE LADDER.

CORPORATE 3-LEGGED STOOL.

It appears that your career has hit a plateau.

Having pieces of the broken cork floating in the wine sort of takes the edge off a romantic evening.

Just a reminder: There are *two* kinds of thermometers.

Two thoughts that, sooner or later, are bound to wake you up in the middle of the night: (a) Death. (b) What you make vs. what pro athletes make.

A fairly unmistakable phone message.

As in comedy, when entering a revolving door, timing is everything.

April 14: Time to make a run for the accountant, or the border.

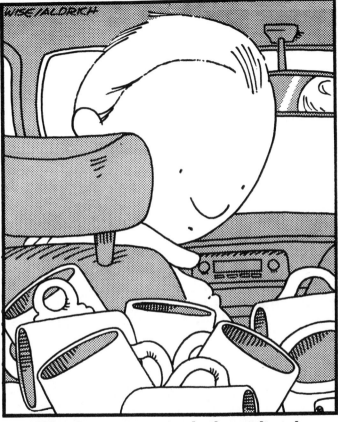

Why there are no cups in the cupboard.

29

The corn people must think that without directions, we'd all just bite into the can.

Either a bold, brazen purse snatcher or another sap holding his wife's purse while she tries something on.

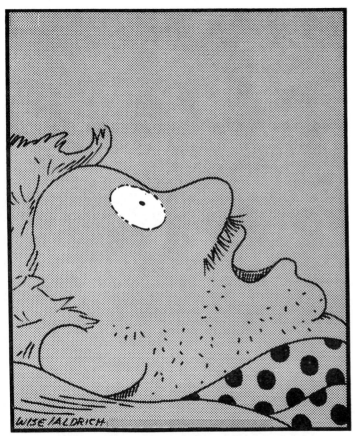

Exhaustive research has proven that what actually wakes us up each day is our own morning breath.

31

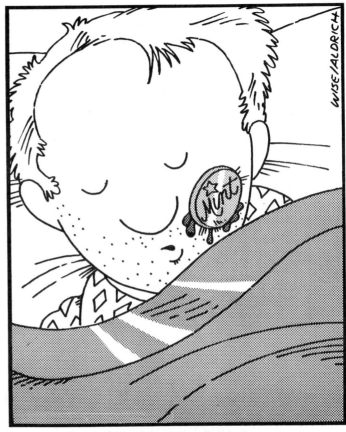

One of the hazards of staying at a really good hotel.

"Clean" and "hide." Another of those cases where words are spelled differently but mean the same thing.

Swimming is much like life. The older you get, the more hesitant you are just to jump right in.

CONVERSATIONS
AT THE
HARDWARE STORE
CAN GET
PRETTY
TECHNICAL.

There are just certain times when a person needs to be alone to work things out.

It'll be the only thing smiling on the course today.

34

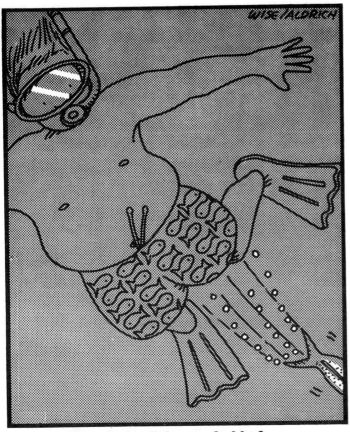

No wonder fish are afraid of us.

There's nothing quite like living near the water.

Male logic: *Real* men always tighten tops
so only *real* men can get them off.

There's a basic flaw in the logic of spending $300
for a machine that can find a quarter in the sand.

36

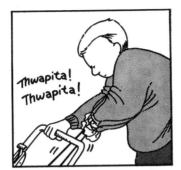

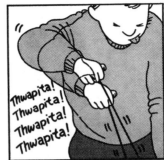

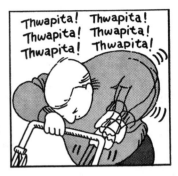

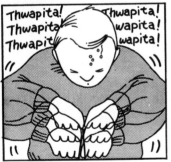

THE POINT AT WHICH YOU SERIOUSLY CONSIDER A HERD OF GOATS.

The consequences of locking yourself out are nothing compared to the consequences of getting back in.

HELL.

RIGHT FIELD.

Where you go if you're bad.

Even the most spellbinding book loses something when read at the rate of two paragraphs per night.

Just what sort of hands *are* those bowling balls at the bowling alley drilled for?

One of the drawbacks of teaching your dog to fetch.

If you park it, they will come.

Playing charades: one of those times when you hope "60 Minutes" doesn't show up.

There are some items you always hope you're not sent to the store to get.

Time to start putting off until summer all those home improvement projects you were putting off until spring.

A roller coaster is just like the stock market: It goes up. It goes down. It makes you sick.

ALL THE PHRASES YOU'LL EVER NEED TO CARRY ON A CONVERSATION IN ANY ELEVATOR ANYWHERE.

First tee thoughts: head down, knees bent, grip firm but relaxed, try not to miss ball.

At last, a sport that makes professional wrestling look intelligent.

Gray hair is hereditary. You get it from your children.

You don't need extra attic insulation. You already have 3½ feet of suitcases and boxes.

Love is never having to ask if you can use his razor to shave your legs.

Look on the bright side: You didn't get the table by the kitchen this time.

1. TABLE LEG. ☑

2. SHOE. ☑

3. DOG DISH. ☑

4. PLANT. ☑

5. COFFEE MAKER. ☑

6. CLOSET. ☑

7. COAT POCKET. ☑

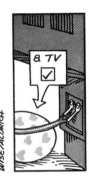

8. TV ☑

9. DRAPES. ☑

10. BOOK SHELF. ☑

11. DRAWER. ☑

12. HEAT REGISTER. ☐

DON'T WORRY, YOU WON'T HAVE TO FIND THAT LOST TWELFTH EGG. IT'LL FIND YOU.

Some days it seems the only thing holding
your life together is sticky notes.

Today is either the first day of the rest of your
life, or just Thursday.

48

**To the weatherman, it means a rainy day.
To you, it means a bad hair day.**

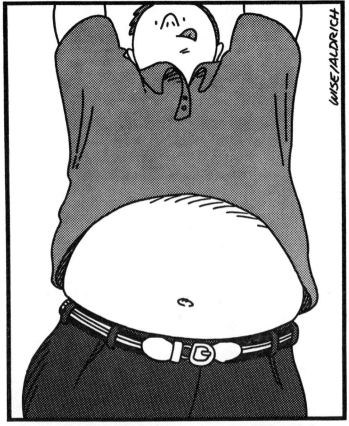

Some things should never see the light of day.

49

It takes longer to put a baby seat in the car than it does to have a baby.

Credit-card calling: It's as simple as dialing 25 numbers in a row in a matter of seconds without getting any of them wrong.

The children may leave home, but their laundry keeps coming back.

**Women separate into colors.
Men separate into "filthy" and "clean."**

A good meeting is just a bad meeting that could have gone worse.

The nonchalantly-strolling-by-the-office-acting-like-you're-not-peering-in-trying-to-see-what's-going-on-in-there walk.

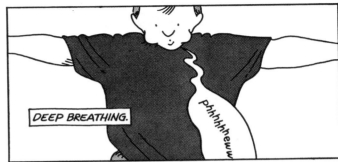

STRESS
RELIEF
TECHNIQUES.

Baggage claim: Denver   Baggage claim: Minsk

**Workaholics need vacations, too.
They just have trouble taking them.**

Applied physics.

How experts choose wine.

How the rest of us choose wine.

Marriage is about love, mutual respect, and picking each other's pockets every morning looking for a couple of extra bucks.

Fantasy Island.

Reality Island.

57

An unfortunate title for a person to whom you entrust your money.

The penalty for passing a cute check should be as steep as the one for passing a bad check.

58

Can't find time to exercise? Get that heart rate up right at your desk!

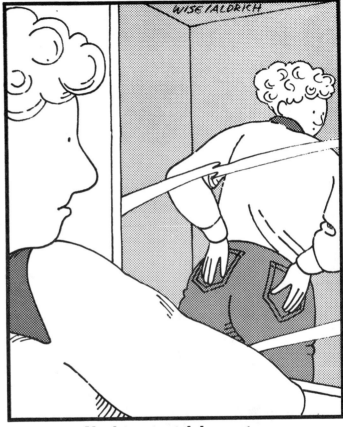

You're not retaining water. You're retaining mashed potatoes and gravy.

Fall.

Fall: when the prudent begin the search for the other galosh.

LAUGH
AND THE
WORLD LAUGHS
WITH YOU.
SNORE
AND YOU SLEEP
ALONE.

The annual decision: Reseed or pave.

How mind over matter works: If you don't mind, it doesn't matter.

The fake-rock house key hiding place:
Unfortunately, burglars get the
same catalogs you do.

Try not to think about the fact that you have just
let someone about whom you know nothing get
behind you with really sharp scissors.

If you can't get the ink to come out of your pen, just stick it in your pocket.

Ties say a lot about a person.

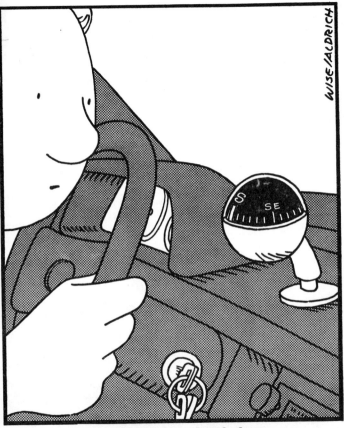

**You may be hopelessly lost.
But thanks to your car compass, by golly,
you know you're facing south.**

**Maybe the reason so many kids have a lack of
direction is that their hats are on backward.**

65

Things only dogs can hear: Somewhere, miles away, a potato chip bag is being opened.

Only the fact that poodles are too short to see in the mirror keeps them from killing us in revenge.

67

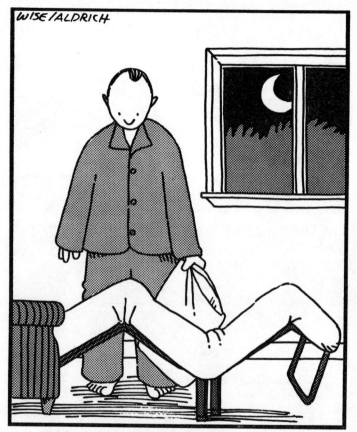

Sleep sofas apparently were named by someone who never slept on one.

68

Often, when people have known each other for a long time, they can communicate without saying a word.

**Male bonding: going to the game together.
Female bonding: going to the restroom
at the game together.**

**Man's worst fear: accidentally wandering
into the lingerie department.**

When you get a really good parking space, you kind of hate to leave.

Fax machine technology transmits urgent messages in seconds so they can lie curled up in the fax basket for days.

IF ALIENS
LANDED IN
THE WINTER,
WHO'D KNOW?

WISE/ALDRICH

You might be too mature to trick-or-treat.
But you're not too mature to pick through the
candy after the trick-or-treaters go to bed.

Cat television. The bird channel.

While not all of us are worth our weight in gold, some of us are worth our weight in potatoes.

Things you know are true but can't prove: The drive-through speaker *isn't* really hooked up. They *are* just handing out random bags of food.

73

**Where you think
you put it.**

Where you really put it.

**Your handwriting says a lot about you.
If you're lefthanded, it says you drag your
hand through what you write.**

30 relatives, 30 pounds of raw meat, no propane.

Don't worry about looking bad at your high school reunion. You can't possibly top how bad you looked in high school.

Obscene phone call.

Getting the snow off the driveway is easy compared with getting it off the shovel.

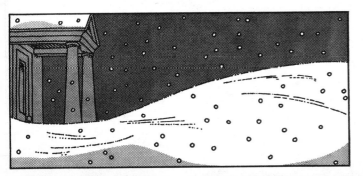
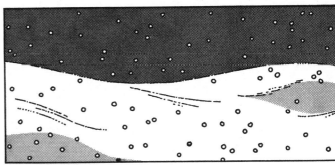
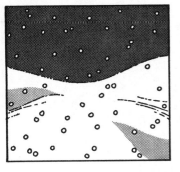
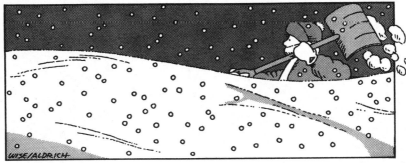

DEPRESSING THOUGHT: 1/12 OF YOUR LIFE IS SPENT IN FEBRUARY.

WISE/ALDRICH

Ah, the smooth richness of sour cream. The pungent bite of chives. The 6-volt zap of aluminum foil embedded in your baked potato.

78

Looks like the folks at the IRS have finally gotten to your return.

Portable sewing machines are portable in much the same way as, say, a mobile home is portable.

Not all money laundering is done by organized crime.

Does it ever strike you as ironic that the people who get to board the plane first are small children and executives?

The only difference between a perennial and a weed is the price.

80

DON'T THINK OF IT AS BRINGING WORK HOME AND NOT DOING IT. THINK OF IT AS TAKING YOUR PAPERS FOR A RIDE IN YOUR BRIEFCASE.

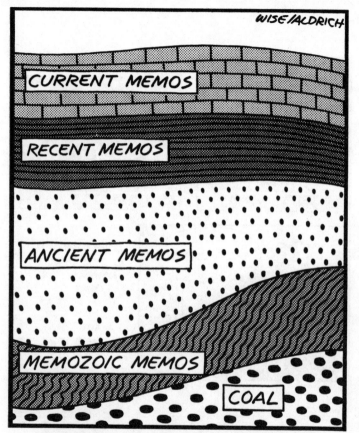

Somewhere at the bottom of your desk,
old memos are being pressed into coal.

There comes a time when you don't just need
glasses. You need glasses to find your glasses.

Another coffee to go.

Suction-cup animals, like many things, are best in moderation.

You'll remember the mop. But you'll have to go back down for the pail, the pail, the pail.

In the '90s, mankind will be introduced to strange new technology and ideas.

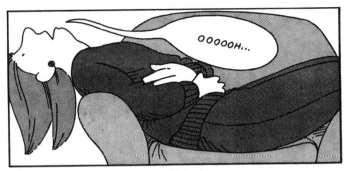

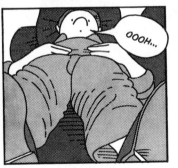

THE BODY IS 98% WATER.

EXCEPT AFTER THANKSGIVING, WHEN IT'S 98% TURKEY.

Perhaps greeting cards are becoming a tad overspecialized.

□ Covers 500 square feet of anything that comes within 500 square feet of it.

GREAT
PHILOSOPHERS.

Out of the loop. **Way out of the loop.** **Doesn't know there is a loop.**

The problem with setting your watch ahead so you won't be late is that you're way too smart to be fooled by a cheap trick like that.

88

Another morning of staring into the closet, hoping against hope that something washed and ironed itself while you slept.

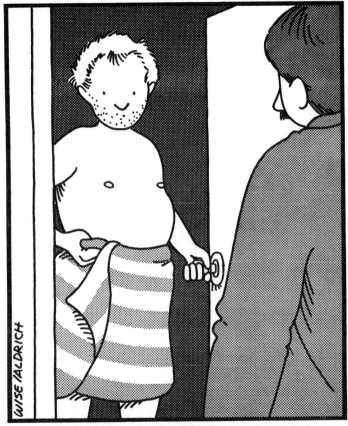

Getting there early allows you to spend extra time with your hosts.

89

You're in real trouble when the extent of your computer knowledge is being able to identify the one in the room.

Cup holders: where to keep your beverage until you're ready to hit a bump just as you take your drink.

90

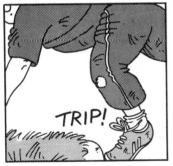

DON'T THINK OF IT AS JOGGING 4 MILES. THINK OF IT AS PAYING FOR 1 TABLESPOON OF PEANUT BUTTER.

It's not a glove compartment. It's a melted cassettes-candy bars-and-lipstick incubator.

The doctor's waiting room: where you trade what you have for what somebody else has while you wait.

92

A FEDERAL
MEDIATOR
STEPS IN,
JUST IN TIME,
ON ANOTHER
BITTER,
HARD-FOUGHT
PIZZA ORDER
NEGOTIATION.

Monopoly games don't end when one person wins. They end when one person's hotels are kicked into the next room.

Marking "fragile" on your package assures it will be thrown underhand, instead of pitched overhand.

The overdraft notice always arrives on Saturday.
Who says bankers don't have a sense of humor?

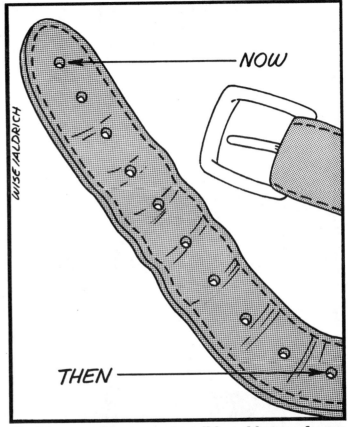

Nothing provides more tangible evidence of your
personal growth than your belt holes.

"... and the award for best smiler and waver in a family home movie or video goes to ... the envelope please ..."

Getting malled: The spelling may be different, but the effect is the same.

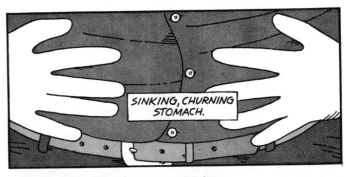

JUST IN CASE YOU'VE FORGOTTEN WHAT SCHOOL WAS LIKE, EVERY FOUR YEARS YOU GET TO TAKE THE DRIVER'S LICENSE WRITTEN EXAM.

News anchors: people who are paid buckets of money for moving their lips when they read.

You think it's dog obedience school. They think it's a dog dating service.

Summer is officially over when you clean the bugs out of the porch light.

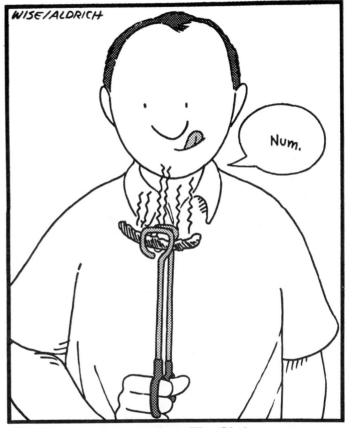

The Thanksgiving turkey. The Christmas goose. The Labor Day burnt wienie.

SOME PEOPLE ACTUALLY DO GET TO BE WHAT THEY WANTED TO BE WHEN THEY GROW UP. LAWYERS, FOR INSTANCE.

Judging by your bills, whoever ran up the national debt used your credit cards to do it.

The best time to put a stamp on the envelope is _before_ you drop it in the mail box.

The horror of discovering the cold, headless body of a chocolate bunny in your refrigerator months after its Easter demise.

A really, really scary Halloween costume.

102

Radar detector: A handy instrument that beeps to let you know in advance that you're going to get a speeding ticket.

WINGED LION
—ANCIENT ASSYRIA

TEMPLE OF RAMSES II
—ANCIENT EGYPT

DISCOBOLOS
—ANCIENT GREECE

BUTTS IN THE FLOWER BED
—MODERN AMERICA

CIVILIZATION SURE HAS COME A LONG WAY.